Blairsville High School Library

P9-DCZ-705

BASIC TRAINING

A Portrait of Today's Army

BASIC TRAINING

A Portrait of Today's Army

by Burnham Holmes

photographs by Dick Frank

★ ★ ★

Four Winds Press   New York

I would like to thank all the commissioned and non-commissioned officers I met, especially Colonel Patrick Vitello and Sergeant Antoinette Loften, and all the trainees I watched and talked to going through Basic Training in the summer of '77. I would also like to thank my editor, David Reuther, for his invaluable advice and assistance.

Library of Congress Cataloging in Publication Data

Holmes, Burnham. Basic training.
1. Military education—United States—Basic training.
2. United States. Army—Military life. I. Title.
U408.3.H62 355.5'4'0973 78-22128
ISBN 0-590-07528-4

Designed by Suzanne Haldane

Published by Four Winds Press
A division of Scholastic Magazines, Inc., New York, N.Y.
Text copyright © 1979 by K. Burnham Holmes
Photographs copyright © 1979 by Richard Frank
All rights reserved
Printed in the United States of America
Library of Congress Catalog Card Number: 78-22128
1 2 3 4 5 83 82 81 80 79

For my parents, Kenneth and Imogene Holmes,
who twice saw me off to Basic Training.

Basic Training is a factory. We feed a kid into a hopper, turn a crank, and seven weeks later we spit out a trooper.

—A COLONEL IN THE U.S. ARMY

Basic is very competitive for a trainee. You want to prove to others, and yourself, that you can do it. And you feel good when you do. That's the best thing about Basic: feeling good about yourself.

—A TRAINEE

⭐ Leaving Home

Your left, your right, your left, your right; I wish I was back on the block.

It is late at night when Jeff and his family leave the house. Jeff puts his suitcase in the trunk and slides behind the wheel of the family car. His father is in the front seat; his mother and older brother are in the back.

At the bus station the Baker family waits in uneasy silence until they hear the loudspeaker: "Now leaving at Gate Three. . . . " It is the bus for the army post. Jeff leans over to kiss his mother. "I'll be all right, Mom. Don't worry."

"Don't forget," says his brother, "you only have one left foot."

Jeff holds out his hand to his father, who grasps it. Then, on impulse, he kisses Jeff for the first time in years. Surprised and a little embarrassed, Jeff realizes what a big step he is taking.

Looking out the bus window at the dim outline of the city disappearing behind him, Jeff wonders what he is getting himself into. He is a little bit scared, but in a way, he is looking forward to it, too. He can't go back home a loser. This is his chance to prove he can make it.

"WELCOME," greets a sign. "WE TRAIN PROFESSIONAL SOLDIERS." Jeff steps off the bus and stares at the army post; with its sidewalks and trees, buildings and houses, churches and post office, golf course and swimming pool, it is like a small city. But it isn't like any place Jeff has ever seen before. The faded yellow buildings are mostly one story, the streets have different names but they all look the same, and everything has the washed-out look of a photograph left out too long in the sun.

Now that Jeff has arrived, he doesn't know what to do next. For a moment, he stands and watches the lines of people getting on and off the buses. Some are in uniform, on their way to report for duty. Others are in street clothes, on their way to relax.

"Basic Training personnel report to the reception station," a man in uniform tells Jeff. "Military transportation is available by picking up the phone over there." Just as people in the military are noticeable to civilians, Basic trainees are obvious to people in the military.

The reception station is a large one-story building that looks like a school. "Let's see your orders, trainee!" demands a sergeant at the front desk. It is the first time Jeff has been called a trainee. "Congratulations!" says the sergeant. "You got here on the right day. Now let's see if the rest of your unit can do the same." Jeff looks confused. "Look at your orders, Private. Your unit is listed right there. You'll be with them the whole time you're in Basic. Right now you're about to start what we call 'fill week.' There are certain things you have to get squared away before you can start Basic bright and early on Friday morning. A-ten-hut! Left face . . . follow the arrows on the floor . . . march!"

The next several hours are filled with all the things that someone at the Department of the Army has determined make a trainee ready for Basic Training. Most important, it seems, is the ability to stand in line.

Jeff stands in line for a haircut. When it is his turn, he is barely in the chair when the hair on the right side of his head is sheared off. (The army barbers no longer shave heads; men are left with a quarter-inch of hair on the scalp; for women, hair is not to go below the collar of the uniform.) In a few more seconds, with the job done, the barber turns on a laugh box. Jeff grins sheepishly at the hysterical mechanical laughter. He looks young and feels vulnerable.

Jeff stands in line for the clothes he will need: boots, gloves and shoes, green socks, green underwear and green towels, four sets of

7

green fatigues, two green caps, two green belts, a green fatigue jacket, and a green duffel bag to carry it all in. Everywhere he looks he sees green. Jeff is growing to hate that color. As his brother predicted: "You will overdose on olive drab."

Along with the other recent arrivals, Jeff is marched over to a mess hall for his first army chow. It isn't as grim as he thought it would be. Each table is covered with a canvas tablecloth and topped with a plastic flower. And for lunch there is roast beef or a pork chop, salad, rice, broccoli, cake, and ice cream.

In the afternoon Jeff stands in lines to see if he will require any dental work, any eyeglasses; he stands in line to receive shots to prevent tetanus and typhoid.

Jeff stands in line to fill out the paperwork for exemptions, allotments, beneficiaries, and benefits. He stands in line to review his contract and to check that everything is in order. He stands in line to have all his records reviewed and placed in a brown manila folder called a 201 file. He holds this profile of his military career as firmly and gingerly as he will one day carry a live grenade.

Jeff stands in line for an eighty-dollar advance on his monthly pay. He stands in line to throw away any "weapons, drugs, and the like" into an Amnesty Box. "No questions asked." And he stands in line for identification cards and dog tags. The dog tags more than anything else make him feel like he is in the army.

And finally, Jeff stands in line at the PX, the Post Exchange, to buy a razor, razor blades, soap, face cloth, and towels. These things are not just practical; they are to be neatly arranged in his footlocker—the wooden box at the end of his bed—subject to inspection at any time.

"Don't forget the shoe polish," says the person behind the cash register. "I hear you're going to need it."

"Okay, trainees, listen up. I'm the drill sergeant of 1st Platoon, Delta Company, 6th Battalion, 3rd Brigade. Everybody in the right

8 place?"

A few trainees wander off in search of their platoons. During the beginning of each new Basic Training Cycle, there are always lost trainees.

Trainees are assigned to companies before they arrive at the reception station. These companies are further broken down into platoons and squads, with men and women living on separate floors of the barracks. A company has about two hundred men and women; there are three platoons in a company and four squads in a platoon. Each platoon has its own drill sergeant.

"My name is Drill Sergeant Delos, but feel free to call me by my first name. Just call me 'Drill Sergeant.'"

No one laughs.

"Psychologists have shown that you learn better when there's some anxiety present. And what's anxiety? *Fear.* If you go through Basic Training with some fear in your heart, you'll do better."

"If that's all it takes," thinks Jeff, "I'll do just great."

Drill Sergeant Delos stands with his hands on his hips. "Remember, we know everything that you need to know. All you've got to do is pay attention and learn it. And think positive. If you think you can do it, you can. All right, trainees, pick up your duffel bags. You're going home."

★ Joining Up

Since 1973, no one has been drafted into the U.S. Army. Why do people join the army if they don't have to?

"My father was in the army during the Korean War and he said it was a good idea to join. I've been planning on being in the army since I was a little kid."

"After high school I wasn't ready for college and I didn't want to hang around the neighborhood."

"A friend of mine talked me into it. She said the pay was good, she got to travel, and the army would help pay for her college."

"A high-school guidance counselor told me I needed some discipline. And in the army I was sure to get plenty of it."

"I've always been interested in electronics. The army promised to train me."

"I really don't know what attracted me to the army. I just saw it as a challenge, I guess."

Jeff stood in front of the recruiting office—the low building between the post office and the laundromat—for a long time and stared at the poster. It showed a helicopter landing and men in green advancing behind a tank. At the bottom were the words: "Join the people who've joined the Army."

"I'll just check it out," he thought. "Can't hurt."

Jeff walked down a long hallway past the open doors of the navy, air force, and marine recruiters. The last door on the right was the army. He stood in the doorway looking in. What would they think of him with his long hair and sandals?

"Come in, son. We won't bite." Jeff looked over to a heavy-set man in uniform. He didn't know much about the army, but he knew that the stripes on the sleeve of the man's khaki shirt were those of a sergeant.

"Have a seat. I'll be with you in a minute." The sergeant turned back to the young man sitting next to him.

"We would prefer that you finished high school first. We've found that high school graduates make better soldiers. But if you're determined to drop out of school, you can join the army with a tenth-grade education or better, as soon as you're eighteen. And then you can get your high school diploma—we call it a GED or General Equivalency Diploma—while in the army. You would have to get it to re-enlist."

"Oh, another thing," said the young man. "I've got a chance at a job, too, if I drop out of school."

"How much would you be making?"

"Three hundred and fifty dollars a month."

The sergeant smiled. "You would have to pay for your food and rent out of that. If you joined the army you would get $419.40 a month, with room and board and medical expenses paid for. Plus thirty days paid vacation a year."

"All right, let me think about it."

The sergeant shook the young man's hand. "Sure. Drop in again in a few days and let me know what you decide. But remember what I said about staying in school."

The sergeant looked in Jeff's direction. "Come on over and let's talk."

"I . . . I was just passing by and thought I would drop in for a minute."

"That's all right." The sergeant pointed to an empty metal chair by the metal desk. "There's no obligation." **13**

The sergeant wore the big silver badge of the recruiter on his shirt pocket. It looked like a policeman's badge.

"Do many people just walk in off the street?" Jeff asked.

"No. Most are referrals. They hear recruiters at career-day assemblies in school. They see ads in newspapers and magazines or maybe even a notice on the scoreboard at a football game."

The sergeant poured two cups of steaming coffee.

"May I ask you something?" Jeff said, reaching for the cup. "I don't mean it to be insulting, but what do people think about the army? I mean, I used to think one thing reading about Vietnam. But now, I don't know. . . ."

The sergeant looked serious. "I feel that the Vietnam era damaged the image of the army, both within and outside it. But, now we're years away from the Vietnam War. People don't avoid you like they used to."

"But joining the army's not really a popular thing, is it?"

"There was concern when we switched to a volunteer army that we wouldn't be able to meet our quotas," said the sergeant. "But, overall we have."

"I was wondering why people enlist."

"Okay." The sergeant poured cream into his cup and pushed the container toward Jeff. "Are you still in high school?"

"Yes, I'm a senior. I'll graduate in June."

"That's good. Any plans afterward?"

"I don't know. I guess that's why I'm here."

"For someone like you, the army might be a good choice—a chance for you to get some experience, see and learn some new things. Are you interested in going to college?"

"Maybe."

"You know, you can start college while you're in the service," said the sergeant. "The army will pay up to 75 percent of your tuition. Or, you can set aside money in a special college fund and the army will give you two dollars for every one you put in."

Jeff's eyes strayed to a poster of a young woman in uniform. "Are there women in the army?"

"Very much so. One out of every ten persons who joins the army is a woman. And that number is going up all the time. Women even go to West Point now."

"What do they do?" asked Jeff.

"Most every job that men do. There are women in 94 percent of the job fields. They do everything except go into combat. And in this age of equality, women probably will be going into combat someday."

Jeff thought back to the stories his brother and his friends used to tell about the army. "What about Basic Training? I've heard some awful stories about the drill sergeants."

The sergeant nodded his head understandingly. "The days of the sadistic drill sergeants are over. They're gone like the dinosaurs. The difference between the old army and the new army is that they used to tell you; now they ask you."

"Really?" asked Jeff.

"Well, that's not quite true. Basic is still not a democracy, not by any means. But the army isn't all Basic Training, either. You have to remember that. I heard it put well by a young man who returned to see me after being in for a year. He called it a 'rite of passage.' I think that's exactly what it is.

"I think the army is good for kids. Especially for those who haven't received a sense of structure from their family or school. Just plain marching gives you unity and teamwork. You would see it for yourself after only a few weeks."

"But what good would all that do me if I weren't going to stay in?"

"Well, it's true, there's no market in civilian life for infantrymen." The sergeant stopped to sip his coffee. "But you're a changed person. You carry yourself differently; even your thoughts are more ordered. You would have drive and ambition, perhaps for the first time. And when your parents see you again, they'll like what the army has done for you."

"I don't want this to sound like I'm going to join, but when could I go in?"

"You could join DEP, the Delayed Entry Program, now. That way, you could go in when you want to go in, up to a year from the time you joined. We could get you the school you want, tell you when and where your Basic Training will be, also your AIT, that's Advanced Individual Training, which is the schooling for your particular job. You would also know where your first duty station will be. All of these things would be guaranteed by a signed contract. And if we didn't come through on any of it, you wouldn't have to stay in."

"How long is a tour of duty?" Jeff felt as if he was getting carried away with all this. After all, he had been on his way to play basketball when he stopped in.

"It depends what you join," said the sergeant. "There's RA, or Regular Army. That's a six-year obligation—three years of active duty and three years of inactive. There're the Reserves and the National Guard. Again, it's a six-year obligation. Three to six months active duty, forty-eight drills a year, and a two-week summer camp every year."

"So, what's the difference between the Reserves and the National Guard?"

"An individual can be recalled on active duty in the Reserves; in the Guard, the whole unit has to be recalled. But no matter which one of the three you joined, you would still have to go through Basic Training and Advanced Individual Training."

"Well, sergeant. I certainly have a lot to think about."

"Would you like to take the mental and physical tests? You would still be under no obligation."

"Let me think it over first," said Jeff. "It's all going pretty fast for me."

During the next week Jeff talked to a friend of his brother's who told Jeff that three years in the army would do him a lot of good. Jeff wasn't convinced at first. "I didn't believe it either when they told me that, but it's true," he said.

Everywhere Jeff turned there were reminders of his visit to the recruiter's. He saw a bumper sticker boasting: "There's something about a soldier." An airplane over the city pulled a banner: "Challenge, Travel, Adventure—U.S. Army." Even on "The Tonight Show," Johnny Carson came out and said: "Do you know what today is? It's the anniversary of the United States Army. So, if you're going out to dinner tonight, be sure to order C-rations."

When Jeff announced one night at supper that he was thinking of joining the army, the family didn't pressure him one way or the other. They just encouraged him to finish high school first. Jeff didn't really decide to join the army; mostly it was that he hadn't decided on anything else.

The next day Jeff told the recruiter he wanted to take the entrance tests.

"I guess I'll take the first step."

"Great! I'll give you a ride to AFEES. Is this Saturday all right?"

"I guess so," answered Jeff. "What's an AFEES?"

The first thing Jeff did at the Armed Forces Examination and Entrance Station (AFEES) was fill out some forms at the front desk. Jeff was beginning to find out that the army has a form for everything. They even have a form for forms. Jeff and the other applicants followed the green arrows to a testing room. About fifty young men and women were already seated, nervously waiting. It looked like a school classroom, except the walls were bare of charts, pictures, and windows.

"This group of tests is very important to you," said a man in uniform at the front of the room. "At one time I would have said, 'I know you don't want to be here, but do the best you can anyway.' I no longer have to say that. You have all chosen to be here. But I will still tell you to do the best you can. The job you will have, or as we call it in the army, your MOS, or Military Occupational Specialty, depends to a great extent on how well you do on these tests.''

Jeff opened the booklet and looked at the first question:

Which of the following countries is not located in Central America?
A. Nicaragua
B. Ecuador
C. Guatemala
D. Costa Rica

The three hours of tests covered general information, word knowledge, mathematics, science, space perception, electronics, mechanics, and even shop and automotive information.

On any test there often is one question you spend the most time on. The one that stumped Jeff was in mechanics:

If gear A makes one clockwise revolution per minute, which of the following is true?

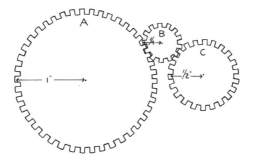

A. Gear B makes one counterclockwise revolution every four minutes.
B. Gear C makes two clockwise revolutions every minute.
C. Gear B makes four clockwise revolutions every minute.
D. Gear C makes one counterclockwise revolution every eight minutes.

In the afternoon there was a physical. (The young women followed a different set of arrows.) Jeff stripped to pants and shoes and had an X ray. He was tested for vision, hearing, blood pressure and pulse, blood and urine. With these results Jeff went to see a doctor.

After a long series of questions, the bespectacled man in the white coat asked, "Do you walk in your sleep?"

"No."

"You know that would really be a factor if you were joining the navy," the doctor said, smiling.

Thirty to 40 percent of all applicants fail the mental test and one out of four fail the physical. Those who failed were told not to think of it as the end of the world. Besides, they could take the tests again later. Jeff was happy to learn he had passed both. The applicants who passed the tests followed the arrows to see a counselor.

When it was Jeff's turn, the counselor said, "I see you have a 'picket fence'—all ones. That's very good, son."

The counselor showed him a book with almost four hundred jobs available—everything from nuclear-power repairman to dog trainer. "Do you know what job you would like to have?"

"Yes. Either infantryman or medic."

"There's a big difference, you know."

Jeff hadn't really thought about it. "If there were a war on, it would definitely be medic. But since there isn't, the infantry might be more of an adventure."

The counselor started writing on yet another form. "When do you want to go in?"

"Anytime after I graduate in June. I'll be in DEP until I go in." Jeff was proud of himself, the way he was getting the hang of things and using the army's tangle of acronyms.

The counselor turned to a machine that looked like a typewriter. "This is hooked up to a computer," he said. "It has all the information **19** on everything that's available." A few minutes after the information had been entered, a print-out appeared. "Congratulations," said the counselor. "Your reservation is confirmed." The counselor told Jeff when and where he would be going for Basic Training, when and where for AIT, and where his first duty station would be.

Jeff then went to be fingerprinted and grilled by an officer on any past police record he might have. The officer did such a good job, Jeff was ready to confess to all the unsolved crimes in history.

Afterward, Jeff sat down to go over his growing pile of records. On top was his contract for enlistment in DEP. He read it over. That morning, Jeff had no idea he would be considering signing this contract so soon. But that was before he had passed all the tests and been promised what he wanted.

He thought it over carefully: "If the army fails to deliver on any of these promises, I know I can get out of this enlistment. And if I change my mind . . . well, it might be difficult, but I could probably still get out of it. I'll have to deal with that if and when it happens. Right now, I want to join."

After Jeff had signed his contract, he was led to the Ceremony Room. It should have been called the Nervousness Room. "What am I doing?" Jeff wondered. "If I go through with this I'll be going off to Basic Training in a few months. I'll have no power, no authority. Just sleeping in a room with a lot of other people is going to be strange." He wished he were going through it with a buddy.

"At this point, does anyone want to get out?" asked an officer in his early twenties.

Jeff was almost sure someone would say something. No one did.

"Raise your right hand and repeat after me:

I . . . [say your full name] . . . do solemnly swear . . . that I will support and defend . . . the Constitution of the United States . . . against all enemies, foreign and domestic . . . that I will bear true faith . . . and allegiance to the same . . . and

20

that I will obey the orders . . . of the President of the United States . . . and the orders of the officers appointed over me . . . according to regulations . . . and the Uniform Code of Military Justice . . . so help me God.

★ Orientation

When I get out of bed,
There's a drill sergeant there.
When I get out of bed,
There's a drill sergeant there.
Drill sergeant, drill sergeant,
Everywhere I go.

Snap. The lights pop on in the barracks.

"Okay. Up and at 'em, troopies!" bellows Drill Sergeant Delos. "Many people on this good earth get up at the stinking hour of oh-eight-hundred and never have the opportunity of seeing the sun come up like you do."

In the military, the day is based on a twenty-four-hour clock to remove confusion about whether it is A.M. or P.M. Thus, seven-thirty in the morning is 0730, while seven-thirty in the evening, twelve hours later, is 1930.

On each floor of the barracks a line of trainees forms for wash-basins, toilets, and showers. Throughout the barracks, trainees make their beds, straighten out their wall- and footlockers, and sweep and mop the floors.

"Son, did you have a fight with your razor this morning?"

"No, Drill Sergeant," answers Jeff.

27

"Well, take a look in the mirror. Your beard looks like you shaved with whipped cream and a stick."

0 5 0 5   The familiar sound of reveille is heard over the loudspeaker. Jeff is disappointed at first that reveille is played on a scratchy record and not by a real live bugler. Also, he had always thought reveille was a wake-up call. It is. But not in Basic.

"First Platoon, all present and accounted for, sir."

"Second Platoon, one sick call, sir."

"Third Platoon, two AWOL, sir."

The first sergeant winces and scribbles the names into his notebook.

"Good morning."

"Good morning, sir."

"Welcome to Delta Company. My name is Captain Todd, your company commander. As you can see, there are three other companies next to us: Alpha, Bravo, and Charlie. All these companies make up the 6th Battalion. The commander of the 6th Battalion is Lieutenant Colonel Murray. Colonel?"

"Good morning, trainees."

"Good morning, sir."

"To continue what Captain Todd was saying, I'm the battalion commander of the 6th Battalion; but our battalion is only one of several battalions that make up the 3rd Training Brigade. There are a lot of people in Basic Training. We're here to see that you become the best soldiers possible."

"Thank you, sir," says Captain Todd. "Trainees, you may think that seven weeks is a long time; but it's short for the amount we have to accomplish. So, starting right now, when you go somewhere or do something, make sure it's with a purpose."

"All right, trainees," says Senior Drill Sergeant Cardona. "Let's do some PT. First rank, two steps forward. Second rank, one step forward. Third rank, stand in place. Fourth rank, two steps backward."

28

Senior Drill Sergeant Cardona first demonstrates then leads the trainees in each exercise. "Army drill number one, exercise number one, the high jumper. I'll count the cadence, you trainees count the repetitions. In cadence, exercise. One, two, three, One, one, two, three, Two, one, two, three, Three, one. . . ."

The high jumper is followed by the bend and reach, the turn and bounce, the squat thrust, and the push-up. Odd exercises except for the old standby, push-ups.

"And now, trainees, a little running," announces the senior drill sergeant.

The trainees line up in front of the mess hall. So far, the chow for lunch and dinner has been things like roast beef and chicken, potatoes, peas and carrots, salad, pie, and cookies. That morning, there was chipped beef, toast, eggs, cereal, juice, milk, and coffee for breakfast. But whatever was being served, many found it funny to be eating on metal trays divided into different sections. **0630**

"I hate having only thirty minutes to eat," says Derek Dorsey. "After twenty minutes of waiting in line, you have to stuff your face in ten minutes. The food's all right, I'm not complaining about that. But I'm hungry all the time."

"I can't stand getting jumped on for talking while in the chow line," says Jeff. Trainees aren't allowed to talk in the mess hall. "It's hard enough adjusting to everything being uniform."

"Or just being *in* a uniform," says Adam Kittlaus.

Although the movie theater where the orientation is held has comfortable seats, the trainees stand for fifteen minutes waiting for the "show" to begin. Finally, the curtains part and out steps the brigade sergeant major. **0900**
Orientation

"Good morning, Sergeant Major. It's a fine day, Sergeant Major," shout the trainees.

29

"Good morning, trainees. The brigade commander will be here shortly," says the sergeant major. "Hopefully, this will be the only time you will see him until graduation, except as he travels around to observe your training. This is 'the old man,' trainees. But the colonel is not old age-wise; he could probably beat all of you in the mile run. 'Old man' is an army term. It means the top; or as Harry S. Truman used to say, 'The buck stops here.'

"When he comes out on stage, I want each one of you standing tall, knees locked, chins back, looking as proud, as alert, as your flabby civilian bodies can muster. And when he says 'Good morning,' I want to hear a 'Good morning, sir' that will wake up your mommy and daddy back wherever you came from. Do you understand?"

"Yes, Sergeant Major."

"What?"

"Yes, Sergeant Major."

"WHAT?"

"YES, SERGEANT MAJOR!"

"That's better. Okay. Here he comes. Stand tall."

A kindly looking man steps through the curtains. He doesn't look like anyone to be afraid of.

"Good morning."

"Good morning, sir!"

"Take your seats." The theater echoes with the sound of over eight hundred trainees sitting down. "I trust that each of you is finding the accommodations comfortable, the food good and plentiful."

There are a few scattered titters after the word "comfortable," but in unison the trainees shout, "YES, SIR!"

"Good. Our mission here is to make the conversion of you from civilians to soldiers. In doing this, we are going to make you physically fit, teach you the basic subjects of soldiering, and instill in each of you a sense of pride and confidence. This is not an easy task—as you trainees can well imagine—but with the help of the good sergeant major here, and the drill sergeants under him, it will be done.

"Do you have any idea what kind of people your drill sergeants are?" asks the brigade commander.

A hesitant "No, Sir."

"Well, let me tell you. They are the elite of the army's corps of noncommissioned officers. They are selected from the best; they have gone through an intensive drill sergeants school; most have been in combat; they are highly motivated and are here to make you into the best soldiers you can be.

"You go through Basic Training only once. Drill sergeants go through Basic many times in their two years here. And at great personal sacrifice, I might add. It isn't easy for them. They are there when you wake up; they are there when you turn in at night. They see ten times more of you than they do their own families. But we feel it's worth it.

"And their reward?" asks the brigade commander. "Their reward is in seeing you go from stepping off the bus your first day to the smart appearance you'll present marching on graduation day. Believe me, you'll be thanking them then. You'll even take over your parents to proudly introduce them to your drill sergeant.

"I might mention two other things. The first is the Trainee Discharge Program. As the brigade commander, I have the authority to discharge any trainee who does not have the proper attitude, aptitude, and motivation to become a good soldier. I will be advised on this by your drill sergeant and company commander. The second is the Trainee Abuse Program. This program is designed to protect you, the trainee, from either physical or verbal abuse by drill sergeants and other officers.

"Well, I've taken up enough of your time. You have a lot to do in the next seven weeks. I hope to see all of you on graduation day. Good day and good luck."

"Good day, sir!"

The sergeant major is hopping mad. "You stand up when the colonel leaves. What do you think happens next? A movie? Popcorn? You will now stand for the rest of this orientation.

31

"Your next speaker is a trainee just like yourselves, except she is about to graduate."

"Good morning."

"Good morning, Private."

"That's all right. You don't have to call me Private." Our "senior" trainee is about seventeen, and except for her uniform, she looks like a cheerleader.

"I'm here because I have three days left; you're here because you have fifty days left. At times you're going to feel you can't do anything right; that everything will get you into trouble. It may not help much right now, but believe me, this happens to everybody. Just hang in there.

"You're going to have classes when you're tired, but you'd better not fall asleep. You're going to go on two bivouacs. These may sound like camping trips, but they're not. All your tents must be in a line. If they're not, they'll all be knocked down and you'll have to do them again until you get them right. And another thing . . . " she pauses. "Out at the rifle range, we had someone who almost shot a lieutenant. When they say, 'Cease fire,' you'd better put that weapon down.

"You're going to do PT—physical training for you civilians—until you feel you can't do another push-up. But when you feel you can't take another step on a fifteen-mile road march, that's when you have to reach down for that second effort. And you're going to be pleasantly surprised by yourself. You're going to find that there's no such thing as your maximum effort. Good luck to all of you, and I'll see you at the war."

She disappears behind the curtain. The trainees are sorry to see her go.

The sergeant major steps down from the stage and starts to pace up and down the aisles. "You may have heard the bad things about going AWOL—absent without leave. Now, let me tell you about the good things. Your pay stops. You don't get paid $419 a month for running away. How many of you remember being fingerprinted? We turn them over to the FBI. Going AWOL is a federal offense, trainees!

"We know where you're going, anyway. Ninety-nine percent of you go home. The local police there will pick you up. And you will have to shell out twenty-five dollars to them for their trouble. Any of you live in Hawaii? The good sergeant major and a drill sergeant will come and pick you up at your own expense."

"If you go AWOL for thirty days, you can go to jail for six months. But we'll still get three years out of you. Your enlistment will run for three years and seven months.

"If you have a problem that could cause you to go AWOL, see your drill sergeant. Or see the chaplain. But don't go AWOL. You won't solve your problems, you'll only compound them.

"Trainees, we are not going to maim or kill you. As a matter of fact, we haven't killed a trainee on this post for twelve years. And we didn't that time, either. The Good Lord did by striking a truck with a bolt of lightning."

The sergeant major lights a cigarette and continues pacing up and down the aisles. "The army does not do things for the hell of it. We gave you more than one set of underwear for a reason. We are not suffering a drought, trainees. Soap and water won't hurt you.

"And keeping your socks dry and clean won't hurt you either. You average twelve hundred miles a year on your feet. If you've got a blister, it'll seem that far just in Basic. And that's another reason to shine your boots: to keep your feet dry. The other reason, of course, is so you can check your brass in the reflection.

"How many of you don't like the chow? Well, it may not be like mother used to make; but mother never had to cook for a thousand people. If she did, she had one helluva large kitchen. And come graduation day, three-quarters of you will have gained weight. The other quarter will have lost. But a quarter of you need to. Last cycle we had a trainee who dropped eighty pounds.

"Now, let me give you some survival techniques. Do any of you like to fight? You'd better forget about it. There's enough physical exercise without getting into fights.

"In the next seven weeks, two of you sitting here will be mugged and two of you are going to be muggers. The army is like any other society, there are always a few rotten eggs. So be good to yourself, don't carry around a lot of money. There's a bank on post.

"How many of you have ever been on TV? Well, whenever you go to the PX you're on TV. Last night we picked up a trainee who stole a pair of dark glasses and had $280 in traveler's checks in his pocket. That's going to cost him $87. You can be sure those will be the most expensive sunglasses he'll ever buy.

"And let me tell you about the nearby town. Every post has got a town outside the gates, and this one is no exception. You may visit it in the fourth week if you get an off-post pass. They'll sell you anything there. I mean *anything*.

"The people you might be fortunate enough to meet in a bar there, they know you trainees are making $419 a month. So, if you're looking for some cozy companionship, try writing some letters home. At least you'll know what you're getting back. Trainees, VD does not stand for vitamin deficiency." The sergeant major waits for the laughter to die down. "We want you to know about prevention and cure. And if you should get a venereal disease, don't hesitate to tell us so you can get it treated. As the ad says: 'Even nice people get VD.' "

The sergeant major stops pacing. "Let me tell you something about myself. When I was seventeen, the principal called me in and said, 'Pal, you and this high school are not compatible with each other.' At that age, I thought my parents were stupid and I knew everything. Well, one night I went out and got into trouble. The judge asked me if I wanted to go to jail or join the army. I joined up, and I'm doing pretty good." The sergeant major pats his stripes.

"Trainees, my drill sergeants' only mission is to get you through
34 Basic Training. If they tell you to do something, there's a reason

behind it. You may not always know why, but they do. You may get mad at your drill sergeant sometimes, but you'd better not tell him to go take a flying leap. It'll cost you eighty-seven dollars. And if you take a swing at one . . . I won't even tell you what's going to happen to you.

"About 10 percent of you here are not going to make it. Some of you quit school, quit jobs, and now you're going to quit the army. The army is no place for born losers. You know those posters? 'Let us join you.' Well, that's not exactly right. You've joined us. There are approximately thirty million veterans in the United States who have gone through Basic Training. Don't you think you can make it, too? Well? Don't you?"

"Yes, Sergeant Major!"

★ First Week

*The first week is filled with administrative matters.
Everything the trainee needs to know in order to make the
initial adjustment to the army. Unit SOPs (standing
operating procedures) are explained for the mess hall, mail
call, sick call, Red Cross, PX, and chapel. The trainees learn
about the wearing of the uniform and military history—to
start finding out how they fit into the big picture. They attend
a seminar on race relations. They begin extensive P T
(Physical Training) and D&C (Drill and Ceremonies). They
serve on guard duty and special details. They learn how to
lodge a complaint through the IG (the Inspector General), but
are encouraged first to go through the chain of command—
their drill sergeants and company commander. And at the
end of their first week, they attend church and a religious
retreat.*

The trainees march to the classroom and stand by their chairs until the
instructor arrives. Then they yell out:

Delta Devils, D–6–3.

We're the best company you ever did see.

First platoon, all day.

Second platoon, here to stay.

Third platoon, all the way.

Around the classroom, television sets hang down from the ceiling. The modern army makes the most of TV as a training aid. Today the trainees watch a film on the wearing and identification of the uniform.

Jeff finds it hard to stay awake in class, especially when the lights are turned off for a movie. But he certainly doesn't want to fall asleep. It wouldn't be so bad if they just got after him; but they take it out on the people around him for letting him fall asleep. That is much worse than if he had to do the push-ups himself.

After the film a sergeant walks to the front of the room. "Most of you are private E-1's," she says. "But if you helped recruit two of your friends, you're a private E-2 and are making forty dollars more a month. When you make private first class, an E-3, you'll be making almost sixty dollars more a month than you are now. So, you can see you have something to work for."

She pauses a moment after pointing to each picture on the chart. "Higher up, there's corporal, an E-4; sergeant, an E-5; staff sergeant, an E-6; sergeant first class, an E-7; master sergeant and first sergeant, an E-8. At the top of the enlisted ranks is the sergeant major. This is what maybe one or two of you will become, if you're an excellent troop—very excellent."

"I know I'm not staying in for twenty years," whispers Adam.

"Kittlaus! Stand at attention at the back of the room." Drill Sergeant Delos doesn't miss a thing.

"For the officers," continues the instructor, "a second lieutenant wears a gold bar, a first lieutenant a silver one. A captain has double silver bars, sometimes called railroad tracks. A major wears a gold oak leaf, a lieutenant colonel a silver one. A full colonel has a silver eagle. Then there are the generals: a one-star general or brigadier general; a two-star or major general; a three-star or lieutenant general; a four-star is just plain general. Don't get all mixed up. A major is higher than a lieutenant; but a lieutenant general is higher than a major general. And the only surviving five-star general, or general of the army, is Omar

40 Bradley. Any questions?"

"Sergeant. Private Errichetti requests permission to speak."

"Yes, Private."

"They mentioned a gig line in the movie. What's that?"

"It's the straight line you make with the fly of your pants, the belt buckle, and the buttons on your shirt."

"Private Baker, Sergeant."

"Yes."

"Are you supposed to salute indoors?"

"Not a bad question, Baker. You salute indoors only when you're reporting. By the way, does anyone know how the hand salute got started?"

"Private First Class Hernandez, Sergeant. In Roman times?"

"That's right. In Roman times, people who visited the emperor raised their right hands to show they weren't holding a weapon. In the Middle Ages, knights raised their helmet visors when meeting fellow knights. And in modern times, people doffed their hats to show respect. Today, we just touch it, because we're so lazy."

"This seminar is on race relations," says the black sergeant, "and I want all of you to ask questions, especially 'whitey.'" There is nervous laughter from two or three of the trainees. "And asking questions goes for the 'jigaboos,' too. And you 'spics,' 'krauts,' and 'slope eyes.'" Everyone is laughing now.

"Do we have anyone from the North here?" A show of hands. "How about the South?" More hands. "The East?" Hands. "And the West?" A few hands. "Are there any here from Puerto Rico?" Hands. "Any Puerto Ricans not from Puerto Rico?" More hands. "Hawaii?" "Yes, sergeant." "Guam?" "Yes, sergeant." "South Korea?" One hand is raised.

"You know what you've just told me? We've got problems."

"How many of you have trouble understanding your drill sergeant when he talks?"

Laughter and grins erupt from the trainees. They are certainly glad that all the drill sergeants and officers are not at this seminar.

"It's not because he's an animal or doesn't speak English. It's just that he's from someplace you're not."

"Does anyone here know what a faggot is?"

"A homosexual, Sergeant."

"No, it isn't. It's a bundle of sticks. In America, we have one word to stand for a whole bundle of meanings. Our society has become a ball of confusion as far as communication is concerned."

" . . . Yes, sir. We've got problems. It may be the way a person talks or the words a person uses. Or, it may be something deeper, more serious than that. A distrust or dislike of someone because he or she doesn't look like you. Or act like you. Or even seem to like you.

"We can't change the prejudices some of you may have in one afternoon—what you've had all these years to build up. It's going to take a lot of work to get these ideas straightened out. But take it from me: They're always based on a lack of knowledge . . . on ignorance . . . and stupidity. Troops, prejudice is just damn dumb! So, y'all had better start beginning to change right now, y'heah?"

"As one 'blood' to another, what did you think?" asks Lynne Allen after the seminar is over.

"There are a lot of us blacks in our company, just as there are in yours," says Derek. "And when we march around we see a lot more. Some of the drill sergeants are black; but there aren't many black officers. How come?"

"Good question," said Lynne. "Maybe we should ask the Secretary of the Army. He's black, too."

1 7 0 0
42   When Delta Company falls into formation outside in the parking lot, Senior Drill Sergeant Cardona tells them to stand at ease.

"You see that sedan over there?" he asks. The trainees turn to look. "That's the general's car. Do you see that man talking to that trainee? That's the general. Guess what happened? Well, I'll tell you; that trainee didn't salute the general. That's right, he didn't salute the general! Trainees, I don't care if it's only a buzzard circling overhead, you make sure you salute everything above you."

"Com-pa-ny," commands Senior Drill Sergeant Cardona.
    "Pla-toon . . . echo the platoon drill sergeants.
"A-ten-hut. Right . . . "
    "Right,"command the platoon drill sergeants.
"Face. . . . for-ward. When I say march, everybody step off with a
    thirty-inch step . . . March!"
    "Your left, your right, your left, your right; I wish I was back on
    the block," sings Drill Sergeant Delos.
"Left flank . . ."
    "Left Flank . . ."
"March. Cover. Get behind the trainee in front of you. Right
Flank . . ."
    "Right flank . . ."
"March. Walk in a straight line. Pick out something in the distance
and walk toward it."

    "They say that in the army
    The chow is mighty fine
    A chicken jumped off the table
    And started marking time.
    Oh Lord, I want to go,
    But they won't let me go,
    Please Lord, I want to go home,"
        sing the marching trainees.

"Com-pa-ny . . ."

"Pla-toon . . ."

"Halt. . . . Stand at . . ."

"Stand at . . ."

"Ease. Are there any questions?"

They might not readily admit it, but many of the trainees experience a thrill doing the same thing at the same time with 200 other people.

DAY 5

1 3 0 0

**Guard
Duty**

"Trainees," says the instructor. "Each of you will be assigned a post to guard tonight. You will have an access roster of the people authorized to enter your area. To challenge someone—I don't care if it's a four-star general—ask the individual to put his or her ID on the ground and back up six paces. You keep your eyes on the individual the whole time while you're checking the ID against the access roster. If the individual is not on the roster, then hold that person until help arrives.

"If you're walking your post and you're approached by the officer of the day, the first thing you will do is halt. Then you will salute. You drop your salute after the officer does. And I can tell you what the OD is going to ask you: your general orders and the chain of command from your drill sergeant up to the post commander.

"But if you're guarding an ammo dump and notice an intruder carrying out ammo, shout 'Halt!' If the intruder doesn't stop, call out 'Halt!' again. Load a cartridge in the chamber and fire a warning shot. Shout: 'Do not move or I'll shoot!' Your intruder will stop. Aim the weapon at the intruder's waist or below and call out for the commander of the relief.

"If the intruder doesn't stop, you fire at the person's waist or below. You do not shoot to kill during peacetime. You just want to apprehend the individual. By the way, here in Basic you will not have a weapon when you walk your post. Are there any questions? Okay. Let's try it. I'll be the intruder and Fedorko, you be the person on guard duty."

44

"Halt! Bang!" says Paul.

"What? You've killed me for no reason. This is no game, people."

Before going on the religious retreat, some trainees from Delta Company talk with Susan St. Onge and Lynne Allen from Charlie Company.

"You know, it feels bad if you don't get mail," says Jeff. "I'm thinking about writing home and asking for a phone book."

"I called my mother last night and she said she hadn't had time to write," says Adam. " 'Time!' I hollered. 'Come on, Mom! How long does it take to write a letter?' You know, I'm beginning to sound just like our drill sergeant."

"I hate to brag," says Susan. "But I received four letters today. Of course, I write letters most every night in the latrine after lights out."

"The first letter I got was from my dad," says Eddie Sutton. "I wasn't even expecting it. He sent me a letter before I even gave him my address. I was just inches away from crying."

"I've cried since I've been here," says Lynne. "It's a great way to relieve your tensions."

"I haven't cried; but I've felt like it," says Derek. "I've never been away from home before. I had it good there: a bed of roses. If I wanted anything, my parents would give it to me. I never had to clean up my room or make my bed. I certainly didn't have to pull KP or latrine duty. I get homesick, that's for sure."

"I'm homesick, too," says Ernest Errichetti. "I really miss my girl."

"Whenever my dad would have a heart to heart with me," says Eddie, "he would call me 'butt' and I would call him 'pops.' When I called home last night it hit me—I won't be living at home anymore."

"Let's face it," says José Hernandez. "You never know how good you have it at home until you leave. Your parents tell you and you laugh behind their backs. Now, I'll tell my brother and he'll laugh behind my back."

Mouth-to-mouth resuscitation

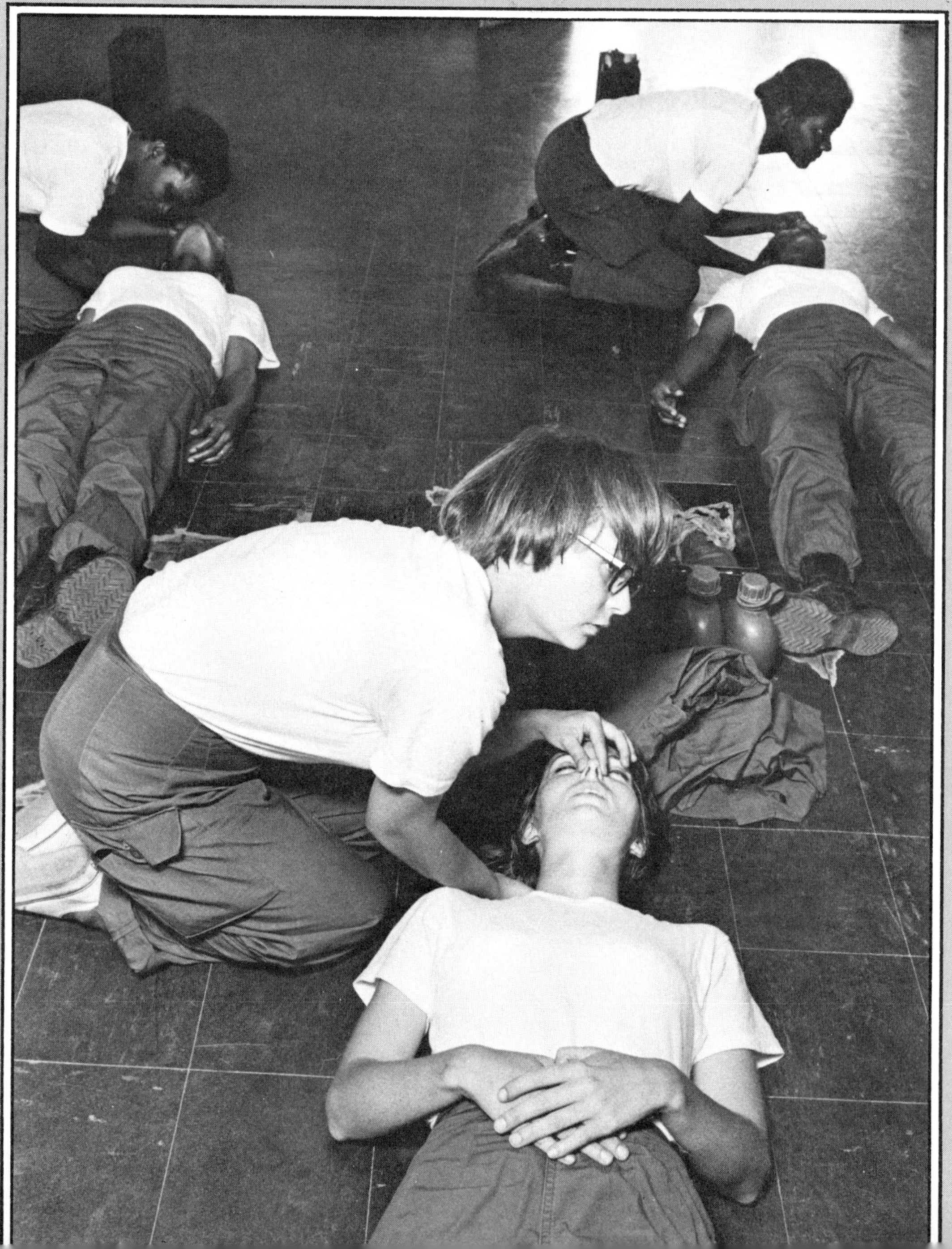

Tear-gas chamber

★ Second Week

During the second week, trainees are introduced to first aid and the gas chamber. They hear about drug and alcohol abuse, how to avoid frostbite and heatstroke, the Geneva Convention and the rights of POWs. They practice safety with the M-16, how to take it apart and put it back together again. They are briefed on military justice and the difference between military and civilian law. They hear about their rights under the Uniform Code of Military Justice. They learn about Article 15, the most common judgment against a trainee, and what Special and General Courts-Martial are. And, of couse, there is P T and D & C.

Delta Company arrives early for the first class of the day and has to wait at attention for fifteen minutes.

"What I hate most is rushing to an area and then waiting for the instructor," says Jeff.

"Hurry up and wait," says Paul. "That's all there is to it."

Finally, a heavy-set sergeant steps forward. "Do not try to relate any of your previous experience to the material we're going to give you. I want you trainees coming through here to have blank minds. I want you to learn first aid the military way. As the old saying goes: there's a right way, a wrong way, and the army way."

The lights in the hanger-sized classroom go out as fifteen TV sets flash on to show a film. Twenty minutes later the film is over and the sergeant begins again.

"That film shows you everything you need to know for mouth-to-mouth resuscitation," says the sergeant as he paces back and forth. "Now the person on the left will lie down on the table." The trainees shoot quick looks at the next person. "We are going to pretend that the only thing wrong with your victim is that he or she is not breathing. Bend down within four inches from your victim's face. I trust I'm dealing here with those things called human beings. If any of you find this funny, you can find your gear.

"I am going to say, 'Inhale, seal, and exhale.' The thing you want to do is get air into your casualty as rapidly as possible. For if you do not get air to your victim in three to four minutes, brain damage occurs.

"*Inhale, seal, exhale.* While you are breathing for that casualty—*inhale, seal, exhale*—one breath every five seconds—*inhale, seal, exhale*—until breathing has been restored—*inhale, seal, exhale*—or until you have been relieved—*inhale, seal, exhale*—or until forty-five minutes have passed—*inhale, seal, exhale*—after this time you can consider—*inhale, seal, exhale*—that your victim is dead.'"

Suddenly the sergeant turns on one of the trainees. "You seem to find this funny. This is a big joke, right? I wonder if you would be smirking if you were staring death in the face? Pick up your gear and get out. And any other comedians who want to join him, do it now."

Many of the others feel sorry for the departing trainee. They have been on the verge of laughing, too, because of the forced intimacy.

"Trainees, if any of you have young brothers or sisters, or children of your own, the breathing method is the same except you puff out your cheeks and puff in air into the child's lungs. This is called the tongue-in-cheek method."

A revolving duty roster is kept for two nighttime jobs: fire guard and CQ, or Charge of Quarters (sort of a barracks secretary). But the most

Blairsville High School Library

disliked job of all is to be on KP. Even trainees who will go to cooking school after Basic dread being on the Kitchen Police. Because a day on KP can be seventeen hours long and feature not only mopping and sweeping, scrubbing and scouring, but also cleaning out smelly grease traps.

"During this block of instruction we're going to learn to drill using the M-16. Trainees, the M-16 is not a gun; a gun is for fun, for sport. The M-16 here is a weapon. It will save your life; it will save the lives of your buddies. This M-16 here is your best friend. Don't you ever forget it. Now, I need a volunteer. Baker, front and center. . . .

"Demonstrator, a-ten-hut." Drill Sergeant Delos unfolds his collapsible pointer. "This is the position of Order Arms while standing at attention. Port Arms is a two-count movement. At the count of one, point the muzzle toward the sky. Keep the weapon diagonally across the body, arm parallel with the ground. At the count of two, bring the arm down next to your hip.

"All together now . . . **port harms!** One-two . . . **order, harms!** One-two-three-four. Keep your elbows into your sides. Don't slam your weapon down!

"**Right shoul-der, harms!** One-two-three-four. **For-ward, harch!** Your left; your left; your left, right, left. Your left, right," sings out Drill Sergeant Delos.

   "**Looking good.**"
"Your left, right."
   "**We oughta be in Hollywood.**"
"Column left, **harch!**"

DAY 11
0730

Drill &
Ceremonies

What does every trainee remember about Basic Training? One sure bet would be the drill sergeants. Another would be the gas chamber exercise.

DAY 12
1400
53

The trainees of Delta Company have been told how bad it is by another company who have gone through it the day before. This kind of information isn't always reliable—the Delta Devils have been misled on other occasions—but still, they are uneasy as they take their seats.

"NBC does not stand for a TV network," begins the instructor. "It means nuclear, biological, and chemical. This is perhaps the most devastating type of warfare."

Jeff finds it hard to pay attention as the different gases are discussed. All his thoughts are on the concrete building at the edge of the field.

"Now take out your protective masks," commands the sergeant. Jeff puts on his mask, clears it, and squints through bleary lenses. The army has a way, thinks Jeff, of changing the English language. A gas mask is called a protective mask. A gun is a weapon. Even something as commonplace as a bathroom is a latrine.

Delta Company is led outside. "When you're in the chamber," they are told, "you will state your name, rank, and date of birth. You will say that information *after* you have taken off your protective masks. You're not going to be able to feel the gas, taste it, or smell it, but you'll know it."

"Oh, no," murmurs Paul. "This is crazy!"

They line up in front of the green building and go in ten at a time. "It can't kill you," Jeff remembers the instructor saying. "It's only CS, the same gas used in riot control. In fact, you could live in there for a total of seven days; that is, if you could stand it that long."

Jeff walks in with his squad. A candle is burning, giving off an eerie glow. On command, they take off their protective masks and mutter their names, ranks, and birth dates. Jeff feels an intense burning on his sweaty face, in his throat, in his nose. Involuntarily, he gasps for air. The searing pain spreads to his chest.

Then they are led outside and told to run it off. "Don't rub your eyes or touch your face. It only makes it worse," cautions Captain Todd.

54 Jeff joins the others in a wild sprint around the dusty field.

"I never dreamed it would be that bad!" coughs Eddie.

"My nose was running all the way down to my boots!" sniffs Adam.

"I thought I was going to make another door getting out!" gasps Derek. **"Ahchoo!"**

"Is there anyone here who doesn't believe in his protective mask?" asks the instructor.

"No-o-o-o-o!" answer the trainees.

"Get a move on, Park. The last one in formation is going to go through the gas chamber again," warns Drill Sergeant Delos.

Trainee Park isn't the last one in formation. No one is.

★ Third Week

The third week is something called an administrative bivouac. Trainees go through a regular day of training, but at night they sleep in tents out in the field, instead of in the barracks. The main emphasis during the third week is on qualification with the M-16. Trainees start out learning to correctly align the sights of the weapon with a target box. They learn the eight steady-hold principles. They learn about target detection. They practice rapid fire and night fire. Finally, they spend two days on a range for actual record fire. To qualify, they must become "marksman" and score at least 17 targets out of 40. With 24 targets out of 40, the trainee becomes a "sharpshooter." Twenty-eight or more targets qualifies the trainee as "expert."

DAY 15
1 7 0 0

Administrative
Bivouac

60

The trainees of Delta Company sit in a field around the instructor. "Each of you was issued a shelter half. Two shelter halves make one pup tent. In 'admin' bivouac, tents will be placed in platoon formation, dress right dress, one helmet liner apart. You position the door of your pup tent toward the enemy so that if you hear firing during the night, you will be in a position to return it. Okay. Get up and let's try it."

The army method of instruction—to explain it and then do it—is conditioned learning. "On-hands training," they call it. There are no points awarded for new approaches to old situations. There is not

much room for creativity. The fathers of the trainees would find a great deal familiar in the Basic Training of today's soldier.

Some people say Basic Training is much different than it used to be, that during the Vietnam War it was more physical whereas now the emphasis is on education. But Basic is still playing back what you've learned. Although issued pocket notebooks, called "SMART books," few trainees find a need to use them.

"If you don't understand something, ask questions. Don't miss the boat. If you miss the boat, you'll sink," the instructor says to the row of trainees lying on the ground. The trainees are lining up the front and rear sights on a target 25 meters away. Behind each target is a fellow trainee ready to mark the target where the aimer sees the cross hairs of the sights meet. The trainees don't shoot at this target, but discover the proper settings of windage and elevation for their M-16s.

"Now aim right at the bottom of the bull's eye and when you get three sightings, draw lines to each. This is your shot group. Okay. Let's get started."

"You started out good," said Ernest, holding the pencil to the target. "But now you're getting worse. Take your time."

"Don't mark it there, you dummy," says Paul, who was doing the sighting.

"Don't call me a dummy," says Ernest. "You made a fist and that means mark it."

By the third week the trainees have heard the drill sergeants and instructors often enough to know what is expected of them. The trainees are familiar with the routine—what needs to be done to do well or just to get by. Some begin to help each other, others to criticize. In short, a few of the trainees are beginning to get on each others' nerves.

"Your shot group should be smaller," says Drill Sergeant Delos, walking by. "What we really want is one shot on top of another, or at least no farther apart than the eraser on your pencil."

"Want to try it again?" asks Ernest. "I'll mark another shot group for you. We've got nothing better to do."

"Naw," says Paul. "That's good enough for government work."

"Trainee!" shouts Drill Sergeant Delos, who has been listening. "We're doing this zeroing to save you time when we get to the actual range. Also, to save Uncle Sam some money. It's push-up time for you, troop. Drop down and give me twenty."

"One drill sergeant, two drill sergeant, three drill sergeant . . . twenty, drill sergeant."

"Now get back there and keep sighting, son. I know you can do better because your uncle has provided you with some nice glasses on your nose there. You may even get a good shot group before the day is over. If not, you'll do it by moonlight."

DAY 19
0800

Record Fire

Qualifying with the M-16 is held over two days on a sandy range far from the barracks. In the middle of the range is a high tower. The range officer sits there.

"All right," a sergeant says. "Give me the first sixteen firers. Line up one behind the other and count off. Go to the weapons shack and get your weapon."

Jeff follows the others to the weapons shack and asks for the number of his M-16. He knows it is his as soon as he holds it in his hands. Before Jeff began Basic Training, he had not shot any sort of a gun, not even a BB gun. Now his weapon almost feels like an extension of himself.

"Let's go, trainees. I need some bodies over here." The sixteen trainees run with their weapons toward another sergeant. They stand at a table and load rounds into magazines, pushing each bullet down hard against the strong steel spring. "You should have fifty rounds. Three magazines of ten rounds, one of twenty rounds."

They run over to a sergeant who stands near an open-sided shed with bleachers where the other trainees wait. "When you go to the firing line, get into the foxhole and face down-range. Use the sandbag to support your weapon. When you see the glint of sun off a target, aim the front and rear sights at the center of the target. Remember these are pop-up targets. They will stay up for only three seconds. Less, of course, if you knock them down. Now, move out."

Jeff runs past the tower to foxhole number sixteen. **"Keep the muzzle pointed down-range at all times,"** echoes the amplified voice of the range officer over the loudspeaker. **"Scorers, get your person into the foxhole and into a three-point position. Raise your hand when ready."**

Jeff stares down-range. It is desolate—devastated by the fire of thousands and thousands of trainees.

"Ready on the left?"

"THE LEFT IS READY."

"Ready on the right?"

" . . . SIXTEEN, YOU'RE HOLDING UP PROGRESS!"

"Baker, wake up!" shouts the scorer. "This is no place to daydream! Get in position!"

Jeff feels as if the whole world is watching him. His parents and old friends, his squad, Drill Sergeant Delos—everyone is waiting for him.

"Is sixteen ready?"

Jeff's scorer raises a clipboard. **"The right is ready."**

"Lock and load one magazine of ten rounds. Firers unlock your weapons and watch your lanes. Targets are at 50 meters, 100, 150, 200, 250, and 300 meters."

Jeff waits for the glint of sun off the pop-up target, but he doesn't see it until the target is on the way down. His shot ricochets off the sand.

"Don't jerk the weapon," says the scorer behind him. "Use only the tip of your finger and squeeze off each round."

Every few seconds another target pops up. Jeff looses track of how many of the human silhouettes he has hit. He does remember hitting one at 300 meters and feeling good as he watched it flap down.

"Cease fire! Cease fire on the firing range. Lock and clear all weapons.

Pull the four-point firing check. Do not, I repeat, do not leave any magazines or live rounds on the firing line. C'mon scorers, get the trainee out of the foxhole!"

As Jeff runs toward the tower, he can hear the range officer getting the next trainee into the foxhole. In the shade of the tower the CO waits for them.

"How'd you do, Private Errichetti?" asks Captain Todd.

"Eight, sir."

"How'd you shoot yesterday?"

"Seven, sir."

"What's wrong?"

"I think it's my breathing, sir."

"Try this next time," the CO suggests. "Take a deep breath and let it out slowly."

"Yessir."

"Well, don't worry about it. You'll get another crack at it. Go down to the weapons shack and pull some weapons maintenance."

"How'd you shoot, Private Kittlaus?" Captain Todd asks the trainee in front of Jeff.

"Sixteen, sir."

"Great. What'd you shoot yesterday?"

"Sixteen, sir."

"Excellent shooting. Try to help out some of your buddies having trouble," urges the captain.

Jeff kneels down in front of the CO. This is so Captain Todd can run a cleaning rod through the barrel to check for a stuck shell.

"No brass, no ammo, sir," snaps Jeff.

"How'd you shoot, Private Baker?"

"Seventeen total, sir. I just made it."

"Good deal. Go down and get something to drink and eat."

Jeff starts toward the mess area when Drill Sergeant Delos catches up with him. "Private Baker. What were you doing out there?"

"I guess I was just nervous, sir."

"Baker, whatever you were, it looked bad. Your chin strap is unfastened. That looks bad, too. And I'm not a sir, I'm a drill sergeant. Haven't you learned that yet?"

"Yes, Drill Sergeant."

"Give me twenty-five, Baker."

"One drill sergeant, two drill sergeant, three drill sergeant . . . twenty, four, drill, sar-geant, twen-ty, five, dill, sar-dent."

"Is that twenty-five, Baker?"

"Yes, Drill Sergeant."

"Why are you kneeling? This isn't church. Stay down till I tell you to get up. Now, get up."

"Thank you, Drill Sergeant."

"Go ask Senior Drill Sergeant Cardona for a bullet stretcher. On the double!"

Jeff runs toward a group of sergeants. "Senior Drill Sergeant Cardona? Drill Sergeant Delos wants to know if you have a bullet stretcher."

"Private, do you know if he wants a left- or a right-handed one?"

"I . . . I don't know, Senior Drill Sergeant."

The sergeants explode into laughter. "Oh, go eat your chow, you knucklehead. That is, if you can figure out how to use a can opener."

Jeff had thought the idea of a bullet stretcher seemed strange; but then, many things in Basic were strange.

"Sometimes I wish I had stayed in college," says Susan. "I'm just not used to people telling me what to do all the time."

"Let's face it—Basic is hell," says Paul. "You're told when to go to bed, when to get up, when to eat, when to go to the latrine. You're treated like a child. If it weren't necessary to breathe, they probably wouldn't let you do it."

"I don't think my sister would make it in the army," says Lynne. "She can't take orders from anybody. I guess it was my home life that made me different. As the oldest, I was in charge until my mother

1930

65

came home from work. Even so, I have to admit I would rather give orders than take them."

"The drill sergeants seem tough," says José, "but they're only doing their jobs. If they didn't straighten us out, they'd probably get busted."

"Now that I'm over my fear of our drill sergeant, all I want is his respect," says Adam. "To be proud of me is too much to ask. His respect is all I want."

"Drill sergeants cut you down and tell you how sloppy you are," says Jeff. "But then at the end, I hear, they tell you how good you are. I guess they just want you to do better."

2300   Drill Sergeant Delos takes off his campaign hat and sits down in the mess hall with a cup of coffee. It is late and the troops are in bed.

"A good drill sergeant is mother, father, brother, sister, and teacher," he says. "By the third week we'll know each of our people. We understand the nature of the human animal. I've run hundreds of kids through Basic and I've called all but three of them right.

"Trainees like Basic Training to be hard. They have certain expectations. Perhaps it's what they've heard—what their fathers, brothers, or even sisters have told them. Most of them would be really disappointed if it were too easy."

"Sometimes," says Captain Todd, "I'm hard on the trainees and my drill sergeants are easy. At other times, I'm easy on the trainees and my drill sergeants are hard. We'll try anything that works. When Basic Training is over, the trainees often say that the old drill sergeant is pretty good. But the drill sergeant hasn't changed; the trainees have.

"You see that drill sergeant over there," continues Captain Todd. "He's one of the best. Even on down time, when they're waiting around for the next class, he's teaching them about their weapons. But although he gives his all to the trainees, he might not be as good as the drill sergeant of the platoon next to his. The other guy works his trainees hard. When they mess up, he has them doing push-ups instead

66

of teaching them. I honestly don't know which one turns out the better troops. It may be the drill sergeant who has the trainees afraid of him. They might be the better troops in combat. And that, in the final analysis, is what Basic Training is all about.''

Practicing with dummy grenades

Waiting to throw live grenades

★ Fourth Week

*The fourth week features hand-grenade training. The trainees
learn the different types and parts of grenades. They throw
dummy grenades and qualify with live hand grenades. There
is also ITT, or Individual Tactical Training, in the fourth
week: how to low crawl, high crawl, and use cover and
concealment during both night and day. And they learn about
the M-60 machine gun, the LAW or Light Anti-Tank
Weapon, the grenade launcher, and the claymore mine. After
getting a chance to fire a machine gun and a LAW, they're
treated to a combined fire demonstration of these weapons.*

One of the most important aspects of Basic Training is physical fitness.
All trainees are required to reach a minimum level of strength and
stamina, but the traditional Physical Fitness Test is no longer used.

"The post record for horizontal bars is 144 in one minute," announces Drill Sergeant Delos. "Let's go!"

"Wrap your thumb around those bars, Kittlaus," hollers Drill Sergeant Delos. Even if you're weak, you should make two-and-a-half
trips."

"Fedorko, surely you can do more than thirteen bars. Son, where do

DAY 22
1830

**Physical
Fitness
Test**

73

Light Anti-Tank Weapon (LAW)

you think 60 percent of physical training is? It's in your mind. The rest is just an extension of your mind.''

Paul looks down at his bloody hands and wants to believe.

"On line . . . get ready, get set, go," commands Drill Sergeant Delos. "Pay attention to what you're doing in the run, dodge, and jump. All you're doing is making a figure eight around the hurdles and jumping over the ditch."

"What'd you get, Jeff?" asks Derek.

"Twenty-one and a half seconds. I tell you I'm going to make 'super jock.' "

"All right, Trainees," barks Drill Sergeant Delos, "on the inverted crawl, you can come back faster than going down. This means you can cut three seconds off your time coming back. Ready . . . go!"

"Come on, Fedorko. It's all in the head," shouts Eddie.

"Plus your feet and shoulders," says Jose. "Go, you black widow."

"Fedorko," laments Drill Sergeant Delos. "Fifty-seven seconds. You did it. You broke the record for the slowest time ever."

Paul looks down and hides his eyes. "It's okay, Paul," whispers Jeff. "We'll get you through it."

"Are we running the mile for time now, Drill Sergeant?" asks Eddie.

"You better believe it. Remember, when you get to AIT, you'll be running two miles for time."

"Drill Sergeant, what's a good time for the mile run?" asks Jeff.

"Five-thirty."

"Five minutes and thirty seconds!"

"What do you mean, trainee? They're running it in less than four minutes."

74   "In combat boots?" asks Derek.

"You mean you're making excuses for civilians?" laughs Drill Sergeant Delos. "You know the only thing lower than Basic trainees? Civilians. Now, get up there on line and I'll read quarter times. Ready, set, GO!"

"We'll continue having PT a couple of times each week," said Drill Sergeant Delos.

"Do we have to run a mile each time?" asks Ernest.

"Of couse. Running's the best thing for your heart, trainee. It was in *Reader's Digest.*"

"I hear the drill sergeant lives about four miles from the base and he runs all the way to the barracks each morning. Can you imagine that?" whispers Jeff.

"I can see a lot of 'borderliners' right now. Errichetti, you're weak in sit-ups. Sutton, push-ups. And Fedorko, how can you be last in everything? I'm going to have someone take your pulse to see if you're really alive!"

"You trainees are tired, right? But you talked for a good half-hour last night after lights were out. We've got lights out at 2130 hours tonight. What time is that, Kittlaus?"

"Nine-thirty, Drill Sergeant."

After lights out, some members of the second squad sit in the latrine polishing boots. Sometimes it is impossible to get everything done before. 2215

"I used to dream all the time at home," says Jeff. "Now, I just go to bed and get up. I don't have time to dream anymore."

"We spend so little time in bed, it's not worth making it up in the morning," says Derek. "That's why I sleep on top of the covers every night."

"Have either of you ever walked fire guard and seen guys doing PT in their beds?" asks Adam. "You hear them in their sleep bitching back at the drill sergeants. It's weird."

"Speaking of beds," says José, "a friend of mine in Bravo Company says that the bed next to his is jinxed. The first two who slept there went AWOL. And two other guys tried to do themselves in—one with pills, the other off the roof. They were both discharged on medicals."

"To hell with these boots," says Paul. "Let's get to bed."

D A Y 2 4
0 7 0 0

Charlie and Delta companies climb onto the trucks—deuce-and-a-halfs as the army calls them—for the ride out to the grenade range. Jeff looks around at his fellow trainees in full battle gear and is reminded of soldiers in a late-night war movie on the way to the front lines.

In the back, two drill sergeants are discussing women in the army. Once everyone is in good physical condition, trainee performance during Basic Training does not differ markedly between men and women. In fact, during AIT, women tend to make better students. This may be due in part to the higher requirements for women enlistees: They must all be high school graduates and score considerably higher on the mental tests given at AFEES.

"Almost all the women trainees last cycle hit the target every time with the dummy grenades," says Drill Sergeant Delos.

"Yeah," says the other drill sergeant, "but there're women going to West Point now, and that's a waste of time. West Point is for combat leaders. Those women ain't going to the 'boonies.' Until they do, it's a waste of time."

"Did you hear that conversation?" asks Jeff.

"You bet!" says Susan. "The army has been male oriented so long it's hard for a woman to break into the ranks. I corrected a guy in front of the mess hall yesterday and he told me he would never take orders from a girl."

"That's why when I'm around guys I tend to work harder," adds Lynne. "But some guys can't get it through their heads that we feel the

76

same way they do. They make wisecracks about how we should be staying at home."

"What's a pretty thing like you doing in a place like this?" guesses Jeff.

"Exactly," laughs Susan. "I'll tell you, it was a shock at first with all these men staring at us. And sometimes it's hard not to react." She pauses a moment. "But we're soldiers first and women second. Many people think it's the other way around."

"My mother, for instance," says Lynne. "When I talk to her, I can just feel her anger over the phone. But my dad, he's really proud of me. And my aunt told me that I'm doing something she always wanted to do."

When the trainees arrive at the grenade range, they are told it is divided into mock bay and live bay. "In mock bay you throw dummy grenades; in live bay you throw a real M-67 fragmentation hand grenade."

In mock bay, the trainees throw practice grenades from the prone, kneeling, and standing positions. The assistant instructors are busy with corrections. "Sutton, if you don't cock your leg, I'm going to break it."

"Errichetti, you move a live grenade around like that, you'll blow yourself up. Once you pull the pin, you hold it the way you've got it. Now, throw it. No! Throw it like a football."

Then they throw one practice grenade with a small powder charge to find out if they can follow directions properly. The dummy grenades sail through the air with a weird whistling.

Training is stopped for lunch. A truck has brought out the food from the mess hall. After lunch the trainees go across the road to live bay. No one talks. From the thick windows of the control area they can see the five pits behind a concrete wall. The wall is full of holes.

The range officer gives them a short briefing. "A grenade takes four to five seconds for detonation. The kill radius is five meters; the casualty radius, fifteen meters. If you hear the command, 'Grenade,' there is a live grenade on the firing line. Point it out to your AI and he will take the proper action."

"What happens if it doesn't go off?" asks José.

"We had a dud a few months ago. First we get everyone off the firing line. Demolition experts come out, put in a fuse, and blow it up. Then it's back to the firing line."

"First order on line," commands the range officer.

A solemn procession of five trainees, each with a live grenade between outstretched hands, moves toward the firing line.

"Walk fast. Do not run."

When the trainees are in the live bay, the range officer commands, **"Up one."** The AI guides the first trainee through the throwing procedure for grenades.

"Reach up for the hand grenade. Get the proper grip with your thumb on the safety lever. Simulate pulling out the pin. Cock it behind your head. Rock back. Throw it high and hard."

"Frag out," warns the range officer.

The grenade bounces toward the tank down range. A flash of light and heat spreads sideways along the ground like a mirage, followed a split second later by a thundering boom and a mushroom cloud of smoke. There is nothing simulated about it.

"Next up."

It is Jeff's turn. He can no longer remember anything he has practiced. All he can think of is that he is holding a real live grenade in his hands and that he can be killed. He follows everything the AI tells him without thinking and with the command to throw "high and hard," he almost throws himself over the concrete wall with the grenade. The AI grabs his shirt and pulls him down to a crouching position. Jeff doesn't see his own grenade go off, but he sure hears it. And for the rest of the day he can still feel the cold metal of the grenade in his hands. He has never felt so close to death.

Two days later the trainees of Delta Company stand in line to fire an M-60 machine gun and a LAW, or Light Anti-Tank Weapon. "My grandfather used to take me hunting," says Paul to those still waiting. "The kick's no harder than a shotgun's."

Afterward they march over to wooden bleachers, like the stands for a football game. In front of them are M-16s, M-60s, grenade launchers, and LAWs. A whistle blows and range sergeants rush out to take up positions behind these weapons. On command, they begin firing. In the distance, rounds skid off lakes, zing and thud into bunkers and tanks. It is a dazzling show. When this display of firepower is over, several trainees stand up as if to cheer. Suddenly a claymore mine explodes nearby. The blast, almost deafening even with earplugs, surprises them right off their feet.

Settling an argument

★ Fifth Week

During the fifth week the trainees go on a tactical bivouac. For four nights they sleep in tents in the field and are on 100-percent alert until 2400 hours. Even after midnight, someone is up at all times. While in the field, they go through a course in defensive techniques. This is tested in the Hand Grenade Course, and later in Soldier's Stakes. Finally, the trainees go on tactical road marches to learn firsthand the different problems of daytime and nighttime troop movements. There are four marches scheduled in Basic: a six-kilometer forced march and marches of ten, twelve, and fifteen miles.

"We will be going on a speed march out to the tactical bivouac site. A speed march is 160 steps per minute or 4.5 miles per hour. Swing your arms, swivel your hips, and take long strides. Marathon walkers do the same thing," explains Captain Todd.

DAY 29
1 4 0 0

Speed March
1 7 0 0

"On tactical bivouac, your weapon is not to leave your side," announces Drill Sergeant Delos. In front of him, at attention, stand the trainees of the 1st Platoon. "You will even sleep with you M-16."

"And wake up with the barrel in your mouth," mutters Paul.

"What are you smiling about, Kittlaus?" shouts Drill Sergeant Delos. Adam always has a smile on his face. Once when he was told to drop down and do push-ups, Adam got up and was still smiling.

"Place your web gear, weapon, and helmet down and pitch those tents," commands Drill Sergeant Delos. "Don't put your weapon in the mud, trainee. Your weapon is your best friend. Would you put your best friend in the mud?"

DAY 30

0800

Individual
Tactical
Training

While on tactical bivouac the trainees receive a course in defensive techniques. They learn how to construct good foxholes. They set up perimeter defenses with overlapping fields of fire that anticipate every enemy avenue of approach. They learn how to go on two-person patrols and the use of weapon fire and hand grenades against enemy positions. They learn the use of camouflage and how to change it as backgrounds vary and plants die. And they learn how to stay awake—taking turns throughout the night guarding their position.

DAY 32

1000

Hand-Grenade
Assault Course

"This course is good for those of you with an MOS other than infantry," says Captain Todd. "It gives you a feel for what it's like to be a foot soldier."

"On this course there are six stations," explains Drill Sergeant Delos. "If your grenade hits the target area, you'll get ten points. Sixty points is maximum and you need at least 30 points to pass.

"Now, when you're going through the woods, you don't move like you're back on the block. You sneak. You're making sure you see the enemy first. Okay. Move down the trail two at a time."

Jeff is paired off with Adam. As they make their way through the thick brush—their sleeves rolled down, in spite of the hot weather, to protect against ticks and poison ivy—they stop to watch a jet fighter circling overhead.

"Take cover," commands the sergeant at the first station. "This isn't a Sunday picnic. Any aircraft that goes over you should consider an enemy." When the jet screeches out of sight, Jeff and Adam get up and look sheepishly at the sergeant.

84

"Let's pretend you've made it this far without being seen," says the sergeant mockingly. "There's a machine gun nest out in front of you. Your mission is to knock it out."

Jeff and Adam crawl to a nearby log. In a mound of sandbags between trees they can see the muzzle of a machine gun.

"**Cover me!**" shouts Jeff.

"I've got you covered," answers Adam. "Bang! Bang! Bang!"

"**Grenade!**" shouts Jeff as he throws his grenade.

"Okay. Get up," says the sergeant as he writes their scores on their cards. "Watch where the grenade hits," instructs the sergeant. "If you missed the target, how would you know whether to throw another grenade? You were lucky this time. And don't shout out 'cover me.' You're talking to your buddy, not the whole forest."

"Listen up," says the sergeant at the next station. "We have an enemy in the field. They haven't detected you yet, so you can catch them by surprise."

Adam and Jeff jump into a foxhole. In front of them are six silhouettes. "All right," whispers Adam. "Let's throw together."

Back at the assembly area, Lynne Allen is telling Jeff: "On the sixth station I started going the wrong way. If I hadn't gotten down, the barbed wire would have caught me around the neck. As it was, it tore the camouflage off my helmet."

"What'd you make, Allen?" asks Senior Drill Sergeant Cardona.

"Sixty, Senior Drill Sergeant."

"Way to go, Private Allen. You 'maxed' it. How about you, Baker?"

"Forty-five, Senior Drill Sergeant."

"Well, that's 'first class.' Baker, you double-time to chow; Allen, you can walk."

"**Fall in!**"

The trainees of Delta Company jump up and run toward Senior Drill

Sergeant Cardona. Jeff remembers the confusion such a command caused the first week. Now they form up swiftly and silently.

"First platoon, all present and accounted for."

"Second platoon, all present and accounted for."

"Third platoon, all present and accounted for."

The senior drill sergeant executes an about face and salutes Captain Todd. **"All present and accounted for, sir."**

"Tonight, we're going on a ten-mile tactical road march." As Captain Todd speaks, he turns a walking stick around and around in his hands. "We're going to cover 2.5 miles per hour. If you had been a grunt in Vietnam, you would have gone on many tactical road marches. Usually these would have been from a rear area to a forward area. For us, it will be back to the barracks."

A cheer goes up from the trainees. They won't have to spend another night in tents.

"Drill Sergeant Delos will now tell you more about it."

"Thank you, sir. In a road march you will be in column formation, on either side of the road and staggered. Staggered because a bullet could go through more than one of you. ——Listen up, back there. This might save your life some day. —— Also, keep five meters between each of you in column. Otherwise, if we encountered a mortar shelling a whole squad could be wiped out.

"Whether you're on the left or right, keep your weapon pointed out. Your enemy is not in your own unit. At least, this better not be the case. And there's no talking or smoking. An enemy can zero in on noise and light.

"About keeping up; it's not so difficult. If your head starts pumping and you need air, keep your mouth closed and breathe through your nose. You can walk for days like that. And someday you just might have to." He pauses to let the idea sink in. "Stretch your legs out and keep the proper distance from the trainee in front of you. If you don't, you'll be double-timing it all the way. And if you fall behind into the suicide squad, there's a drill sergeant back there who won't be glad to see you. Let's get going."

Delta Company starts off slowly, but soon they are walking steadily down the road. As the road winds through the bogs, the late afternoon sun filters through the choking dust raised by 190 trainees.

At first Jeff looks around, expecting an ambush. He has heard about such things. The others must be thinking that too; they look like the ad for joining the army. But after a couple of miles, everyone relaxes.

Jeff looks at his watch and counts his steps. They are walking 120 steps per minute. Ernest, in front of him, is sniffing what must be a perfumed letter. Adam, across from him, is walking with his eyes closed. Trainees behind him are grabbing blueberries by the road. A jet stream in the twilight seems to pass by the new moon. Jeff hears the clanking of a mess kit. Someone has forgotten to wrap it in a sock.

The second time they pass a log bridge, José laughs. "We're going around in circles. I know we've been here before."

"I heard this post is 47,000 acres," says Adam. "And I think we've walked all of them since we've been here."

Drill Sergeant Delos is right. It does get dark in these woods. And what had started out as a good walk is now getting to be a lot of work. Some trainees no longer keep their weapons pointed out.

Suddenly, the long columns stop. For a moment the trainees stand in the road, then realize they are supposed to deploy in a defensive position. As he hits the dirt and scrambles for cover, Jeff wonders if this is an ambush. But it isn't. It's a rest break; they have reached the halfway point. The trainees get up and file past a lister bag—a large cloth bag of water—and fill their canteens.

In a stand of trees, Captain Todd is talking in a low voice to Senior Drill Sergeant Cardona. He is still carrying his walking stick. Jeff draws close enough to listen.

"I never liked to travel with this many men in Vietnam," says the captain. "As a matter of fact, a squad was all the men I liked to lead. Then your men were hand-picked. You knew them and knew what to expect."

The sergeant says something Jeff can't hear. "The M-16 is a good weapon," continues the captain, "because of all the fire power. But the M-16 wasn't very effective against the 'Cong.' You would hit them and it'd go right through them. Unless, of course, you hit a vital organ or shattered a bone. It was very frustrating to empty a clip into them and they'd still keep coming at you with a satchel charge. They were just like the pop-up targets on the range." As he talks, the company commander leans against his walking stick. "Also, most of your fights were at less than a hundred meters. And in close, the M-16 with its plastic stock wasn't much good. It would just break over someone's head."

As the captain and sergeant walk off to the head of the company, Jeff wonders how many trainees today ever thought about Vietnam. Probably not many.

"Anybody tired?" asks Drill Sergeant Delos. For once, because of the restriction on noise, the trainees don't have to shout back the expected reply. It feels good not to lie. They silently form into columns and move on down the road.

At the end of the ten-mile march the trainees are tired and some tempers are short. There are not that many fights in Basic; usually it's "push and shove" until someone breaks it up. But tonight is different. While Delta Company is cleaning weapons, a fight erupts between two trainees in another platoon.

"Hey! Get off that man!" yells a drill sergeant.

"He called me a 'nigger'!"

"All right! Both of you! To the dayroom! March!" commands the
88 drill sergeant.

The rest of the trainees continue cleaning their weapons. After a while, the conversation turns to other things.

"Before we went on bivouac," says Derek "I couldn't wait to get away from the barracks. But after a week in the field, I couldn't wait to get back home—I mean to the barracks. Never thought I'd be calling the barracks 'home,' " he laughs.

The trainees are marching over to the arms room when another fight breaks out.

"Stop! Stop right there!" shouts a drill sergeant. "What are you doing swinging your weapon at him?" The drill sergeant runs over and grabs the trainee. "You swung your weapon at him!"

"He pushed me!" says the trainee. "Just like you're doing now!"

"All right!" shouts the drill sergeant. "Hit me, trainee!" The drill sergeant, his hands clenched and at his sides, leans toward the trainee. "C'mon! Hit me! Hit me right now!"

The trainee stands looking down at the ground.

"Trainee! Come with me to see the captain!" says the drill sergeant. "You're not long for this army! Now move!"

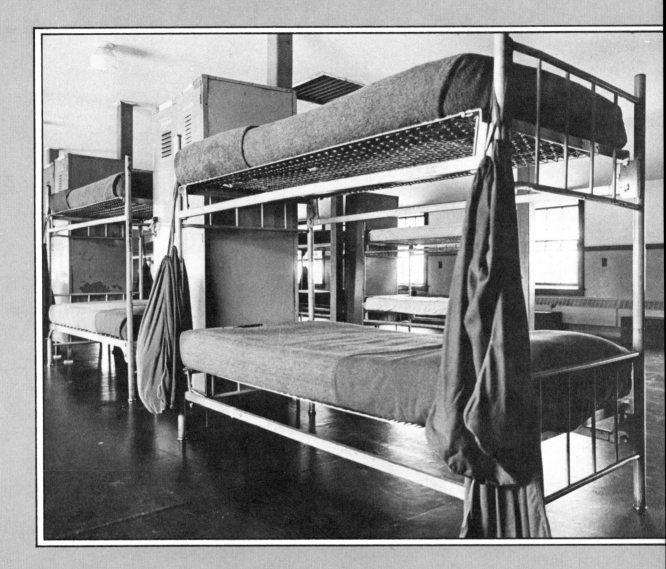

⭐ Weekend Pass

After the third week of Basic, trainees may receive the weekend off; however, they're restricted to the area around their barracks. The fourth weekend they may be given a post pass to go to the gym, the swimming pool, the snack bar, the bowling alley, and the trainees' club. The fifth and sixth weekends of Basic, they are eligible for off-post passes. Time off, a chance to relax after the long, busy week, is important. But a pass is a privilege, and not automatic. It must be earned.

The barracks are spotless the next day. But the CO, sterner than they have ever seen him, only looks at their uniforms. As he moves up and down the ranks, finding fault with almost every brass belt buckle, the trainees of Delta Company expect the worst. Instead, he announces they will all get passes.

D A Y 3 4

1 0 0 0

Inspection

The line at the PX cafeteria is almost out the door. "I never get tired of hamburgers, that's for sure," says Derek to another trainee in line. "Every chance I get I come over here and eat a couple. I could eat them three times a day and on weekends I do. Some people like to drink beer. Me, I like to eat hamburgers."

"Most of all," says Adam, "I miss watching television and reading newspapers, especially the sports section. So, I bought all the papers I could find and checked into a motel in Bordertown that had a really nice color set in the room. I even read the ads and watched the test pattern.''

Eddie spends Saturday evening drinking beer, making a pyramid of empties on a table in the trainees' club. ''There was a band and everyone was yelling for favorite songs. Most of the people were feeling pretty good. You could just feel the excitement buzzing around you. There was this girl, a trainee in another company, sitting with these two jerks. They were so ugly they'd have to sneak up on a mud puddle to get a drink. I asked her to come over and sit with me, the only class guy in the joint, but she refused.''

''This morning,'' says Eddie, ''I woke up with all my clothes on. I looked up and saw someone else's name on the wall locker. I don't know how I got there, but I'd been sleeping in the wrong bed.''

Charlie Company gets weekend passes, too. Lynne and Susan go to a large city nearby. ''We got off the bus and there it was—all those buildings and people. It was fascinating, but we didn't know anyone or where to go. We did a few things; but mainly we just walked around. Then we went back to the bus station and waited for the next bus back here.''

Jeff and José don't do much of anything. Mainly they hang around the barracks—José talking and shining boots, Jeff sleeping. But they do go to a movie both nights. Jeff sleeps through these, too. The air-conditioned theater makes Jeff feel more comfortable than he has felt in weeks.

On the outskirts of any army post there always seems to be a Bordertown. The town generally isn't much—mostly bars, motels, pawnshops, tattoo and pizza parlors. A lot of men and women trying to separate soldiers from their money.

"I went into the Poster Palace in Bordertown," says Paul, "and they took me to the back where they sell diamonds." They talk to you like you were real good friends and shake your hand every thirty seconds. I must've told them a dozen times I didn't have much money, but they gave me all this sad stuff and before I left, two other trainees in there put down payments on pearl necklaces for their mothers and diamond rings for their girl friends."

Applying camouflage

# ★ Sixth Week

There are three things each trainee must pass in order to graduate from Basic Training: Basic Rifle Marksmanship, the Hand-Grenade Assault Course, and Soldier's Stakes. These last two take place during the sixth week. By the sixth week the drill sergeants have changed from negative to positive motivation and things are becoming a little more relaxed. It is a time for making the transition from being a trainee to being a soldier.

"I don't like to use profanity . . ." begins Captain Todd.

"Damn right!" adds Drill Sergeant Delos.

"But this is one helluva company. The Delta Devils beat the other companies in the battalion on the Assault Course yesterday."

The trainees break into cheers.

"I'm really proud of you people!" The CO looks as happy as the trainees. The drill sergeants standing by beam like proud parents.

"Well, I know you people are the strongest and the fastest. We've already proved that. Now, we're going to show we're the smartest on Soldier's Stakes later in the week. We'll do it—I know it and you know it. And next week, we'll all go to graduation and look pretty."

From a distance, the logs, ropes, and tree houses of the Confidence Course look like a giant playground. Yet even the names of the obsta-

cles—the Tough One, the Belly Robber, the Dirty Name, the Slide for
Life—suggest a rough time. This course is a test of their strength,
coordination, balance, and courage.

"On the rope climb I was afraid to go over the top and come back down again," says Jeff. "But Drill Sergeant Delos was up there talking to me, asking me where I was from. Then he told me to swing my leg over. I did and came back down. Oh-wie! Was I ever glad to get back on the ground."

"You know," says Lynne, "things you once thought you could never do, you're doing. Some people froze out there; but seeing others do it, you do it, too."

"I guess you just have to exclude the word 'can't' from your vocabulary," says Susan. "They tell you what to do and you do it. You learn you can get anything done if you put your mind to it."

"But you also learn to work as a team," says Lynne. "If you go it alone, you're not going to make it."

It might also be said that the Confidence Course treats everyone the same. Captain Todd fell flat on his face trying to show some trainees how to get over the High Stepper.

Six at a time they run through the obstacle course—scrambling over
and under logs, climbing a rope and walking across a balance beam,
scaling walls and fences, jumping across a pit, climbing hand over
hand the high cargo net.

The first time they run through wearing T-shirts; the second time in full combat gear. Then the fastest from each platoon race against each other. The first platoon comes in second.

"The hardest one is the cargo net," says Derek. "The net was shaking more than I was."

"No, it's not," says Eddie. "It's the walls. You get such a short run between them."

"On your feet," says Senior Drill Sergeant Cardona to a group of trainees sitting on the ground. "You people have it easy. The obstacle course used to be a low crawl under barbed wire and machine-gun fire. Nowadays, you trainees don't even go through bayonet training."

DAY 38
0630

"Today is the big day," says Drill Sergeant Delos. "You must receive at least a 70 percent at each station to be a 'Go.' Otherwise, you're a 'No-Go.' Is everybody ready?"

Soldier's
Stakes

"Yes, Drill Sergeant."

The trainees' helmets are heavy with camouflage, the sticks and weeds transforming the Delta Devils into a herd of two-legged reindeer.

"Is everybody going to 'max' the test?" he asks.

"We'll get close," answers Paul.

"Close! Close only counts in horseshoes! Can you ace it?"

"Yes, Drill Sergeant."

It starts to rain as Jeff and José run to the first station. On top of a hill is a shed. Sniper fire comes from an open window.

"Cover me while I move," Jeff whispers to José.

"I've got you covered." As Jeff crawls along the tree line to a rise within throwing distance of the shed, he hears the blanks from José's weapon. Jeff unfastens a grenade, pulls the pin, and throws it high and hard. The grenade sails through the window, bounces around inside, and goes off. White smoke rises from the small powder charge of the grenade. It is a direct hit.

The next station startles Jeff and José. Beside an overturned truck are two grotesque dummies. It is shocking, as if they are on a bloody battlefield.

"They've stopped breathing. Take the proper action," advises a sergeant. José and Jeff bend over the casualties to give mouth-to-mouth resuscitation. Rain pings off their helmets. Up close, the dummies seem real.

108

Beyond are two more dummies. "The first thing we do is check for a chest wound," says José. "Roll him over to see if the bullet came out his back. Then we make sure the wound is airtight by placing a bandage on the wound and tying it secure with your belt. We treat him for shock by turning him to the side to make sure the blood doesn't run into the lungs, and covering him with a poncho."

Jeff follows José across a rickety bridge. They carry their weapons at port arms. A sniper opens fire on them, scattering them to either side of the path.

"Cover me while I move," says José.

"I've got you covered," answers Jeff. He fires a blank toward the sniper as José sprints to a rock wall.

"Baker, move out," orders José.

"Cover me."

"I've got you covered," answers José. He fires a blank as Jeff crawls to a fallen tree.

"Hernandez, move out," orders Jeff.

"Cover me."

"I've got you covered."

The next station is a bunker lit by a single candle. "In a war," says the sergeant, "you'll have to clean your weapon in a minute. If your weapon jams, you won't be able to yell for your drill sergeant."

Jeff and José take turns disassembling and reassembling their M-16s. Before, they have always done this in broad daylight. Now, in near darkness, the M-16 at first seems strange and unfamiliar.

It is raining hard as Jeff and José jog down the trail. A sergeant steps out from behind a tree. "Halt! Who goes there?"

"A friend," replies Jeff.

"Advance one at a time and be recognized." Jeff walks to within one meter of the sergeant. "Halt! Golden," whispers the sergeant.

"Dragon," answers Jeff, completing the password Drill Sergeant Delos had told them earlier. After José completes the password, they are given the next situation.

"Your squad has been chosen to cover a platoon sector. You're expecting an attack tonight. Move out and select your position."

José looks at the three foxholes and whispers his choice to the sergeant. Jeff chooses the same one. It has the best overhead cover, and it doesn't have trees blocking the view from the foxhole.

Jeff and José run down a ravine to a small hut. Inside are enemy plans. Jeff enters, suspecting a trap. At the first whiff of smoke, he pulls on his protective mask and yells, "Gas."

"Okay. You can take it off now," says the sergeant, watching through the window. Jeff starts to reach for his mask, then stops. He isn't sure why: After hours of training, it is an automatic response. The next thing he hears is "All clear." Jeff is a "Go." Later, he hears that sometimes trainees didn't wait for the all-clear signal.

The last situation is billed as a use of initiative. A rope hangs from a beam high over the middle of a large pit filled with muddy water. Jeff slings his M-16 across his back and retreats to get a running start. He leaps at the edge of the pit, but slips on the wet bank and catches the rope low. He swings right into the water. Falling forward in water up to his shoulders, he scrambles up the sandbags on the other side to the laughter of those watching. He turns and watches Jose calmly pick up a long branch, pull the rope toward himself, grab the rope high up, and easily swing across.

"You fox!" says Jeff.

José laughs. "It's the small things that count. No matter how brave and strong you are, you need some gray matter up here," he says, tapping his forehead.

110   Jeff looks at his weapon, all muddy. It will take hours to get it clean.

"All right," says Drill Sergeant Delos back at the assembly area. "Everyone in the 1st Platoon has passed Soldier's Stakes."

A cheer goes up from the wet and muddy troops.

"Basic is almost over," says Drill Sergeant Delos. "You may feel so short you could sleep in a matchbox. But let me tell you something. I'm a staff sergeant, an E-6; most of you are privates, E-1's. But I was a trainee in Basic Training, a trainee in AIT, a trainee at Airborne School, a trainee at the NCO Academy and a trainee at Drill Sergeants School. So, pick up your gear, trainees, and get ready to move out."

"Hup, two, thu-ree, fo-wer. . . ."

"Standing tall and looking good,
We oughta be in Hollywood."

 # Seventh Week

The seventh and final week includes something different: sports (volleyball, flag football, soccer, boxing, basketball, track and field) and drill competition. The two areas of drill competition are mandatory (based on the field manual) and freestyle. The best platoon in each company qualifies for the overall brigade competition. Also, there is equipment turn-in and outprocessing: AIT and travel plans. Most trainees go group shipment early next week by either bus or plane. And, of course, there is graduation.

On the day before graduation, some friends from Charlie and Delta Companies are passing by the reception station. A group of incoming trainees, looking lost and bewildered, are waiting to go to their new "home." It doesn't seem so long ago when Jeff and his friends had been waiting there with their duffel bags.

"Hey!" says one of the new trainees. "What's Basic going to be like?"

"My advice would be 'Don't quit,' " says Eddie. "After the first couple of weeks it gets easier and you start feeling better about things."

"Mine would be to use common sense," says Ernest.

"And never lose your cool," adds Jeff. "That's what a drill sergeant is looking for."

"Right," says Ernest. "If you bellyache all the time, you'll get picked on."

"Go in with an open mind," urges Susan. "Program yourself to expect the unexpected."

"If I were to tell someone something," says Derek, "it would be that you can't come in fresh off the block. Be in shape. That's probably why a lot drop out. You've got to have both the muscles and the mind for it. Also, people should know what they're getting into. I never even heard of hospital corners before I came in. Basic isn't like butter. You can't just slide through it."

"Learn to see the humor in everything that happens, good or bad," advises Adam. "If you can't look at things and laugh about them, you'll be in sorry shape."

"I would just like to tell you that it isn't easy," says Paul. "Basic is the biggest mental and physical strain I've ever been through. I've made it and I haven't made it. It's been rough. I don't know what AIT will be like."

"Don't expect it to be easy. Do what you have to do and a little bit more," suggests Lynne. "And remember that Basic Training, and even AIT, for that matter, is not the army. It's designed to get you physically fit and thinking in a particular way. Things will be different when you get to your permanent duty station."

"I've got my opinion," explains Jose, "but if you talk to nine different people, you'll get nine different opinions. When we were at the reception station, we were told about Basic by other trainees. But I never saw any of the things they told us about. Different companies vary; different platoons vary. It's hard to know what to believe. You have to experience it for yourself."

Leaving the new trainees, Jeff realizes that next week they will be starting over again. Most of them will be going to another post for AIT —Advanced Individual Training—that will last anywhere from a few weeks for some of the jobs to several months for the more technical fields. But even so, none of the trainees will probably ever feel quite as lost as they did seven weeks ago.

Delta Company marches behind Charlie over to the parade grounds for the graduation exercises. As the brigade marches onto the field lined with the flags of the trainees' states, families and friends uncase cameras and binoculars. Somebody's younger brother is practicing salutes in front of one of the thirty flags. The band plays and the reviewing officer inspects the troops.

The brigade is ordered to parade rest as the post commander rises to speak. It is the third time—twice from across a field—the trainees of Delta Company have seen the general.

"I would like to welcome all of you who came here today. There are many distinguished guests here in the audience; but the really distinguished guests we have today are the soldiers." This is greeted by scattered applause. "You have completed your Basic Training and are changed persons. You will never be the same persons you were before you came here. And that is good. Congratulations and good luck."

"Officers, colors and persons to be decorated," says the adjutant, the assistant to the brigade commander. Four persons from each company march to the reviewing stand on the other side of the field.

"Sir, persons to receive awards and colors are present."

"Please rise for the playing of the national anthem."

Two bugles sound the anthem. Then the first three companies receive their awards.

"Captain Todd accompanied by First Sergeant Jackson will present the awards to the outstanding trainees of Delta Company."

"The trainee with the highest Basic Rifle Marksmanship score is Private First Class Matthew Lantowski."

"For displaying outstanding leadership qualities, the Trainee Leader of the Cycle is Private Anton van Dalen."

"For demonstrating overall outstanding qualities, the Trainee of the 119

Cycle for Delta Company is Private First Class José Hernandez.''

"There is one trainee," continues the adjutant, "in all of the graduating companies of the brigade who has displayed the most outstanding soldierly qualities—whose spirit, honor, initiative, and loyalty set a high example for all comrades in arms. The Outstanding Trainee Award for the 3rd Basic Training Brigade goes to Private First Class Lynne Allen of Charlie Company.''

"Atta-baby!" half-shouts Derek.

The next award is for the drill sergeant of the cycle, "who exemplifies outstanding abilities to lead, to teach, to guide, to counsel." Drill Sergeant Patrick Sullivan is presented the blue cord by the brigade commander.

"Who's that?" asks Eddie.

"Beats me. Maybe he mispronounced Byron Delos," says Ernest.

"There is one company in the brigade which is awarded the guidon streamer for achievements based on performance in Basic Rifle Marksmanship, the Hand-Grenade Assault Course, and Soldier Stakes, and the number of trainees graduating compared to the number who began. This company is Delta Company.''

"Maybe we should turn 'pro,' " suggests Adam.

"And go through Basic again, right?" asks Jeff.

"Wrong," says Paul.

"Pass in review," commands the adjutant. "Ladies and gentlemen, as the graduates pass in review, we ask that you stay behind the barriers.''

"Daddy! Look!" cries the little boy in front of the flag. "There're women out there!''

At the brigade luncheon afterward, family and friends mingle with the graduates, drill sergeants, and officers. A band is playing "This Is the Army, Mr. Jones." Mr. Baker and Mrs. Allen are taking pictures.

"I know it sounds corny," admits Paul, "but marching out on the field today, I had chills up and down my spine.''

"Drill Sergeant Delos!" calls out Adam. "Come join us for a picture."

"Drill Sergeant," says Ernest, "we're all disappointed you didn't win the award."

"Don't be," says Drill Sergeant Delos. "I've put my thumbprint on you and look how you've turned out. Take Private Hernandez, for example. And all of you. . . . You're part of the best company in the cycle. Of course, none of you can hold a candle to Private Allen. Congratulations, Private. You must be very proud of her, Mrs. Allen."

"When she left," says Mrs. Allen, "every member of the family was at the train station. When she returns after AIT, we'll stretch a banner across the front yard."

"You know," says Jeff, "we've got some memories from Basic. Like when we had to repitch our tents in the middle of the night because of that severe storm warning. And it only sprinkled."

"Or when we were coming back from patrol," recalls Derek, "and Adam called out, 'Halt! Who goes there?' I answered 'A friend.' He said, 'Advance and be recognized.' But after that, nothing. I thought at first he'd forgotten the password. 'Say Jack,' I whispered, 'and I'll say Frost.' But he still didn't answer. He was sound asleep!"

"I'll never forget when I didn't call Drill Sergeant Delos by his first name—Drill Sergeant," says Paul. "I was doing push-ups for half an hour. 'Knock 'em out, killer,' you kept saying."

"Looking back on Basic," says Jeff, "I think we'll all have to admit, it didn't seem so bad."

"Yes, I guess you could say we've finally gotten Basic Training down," says Derek. "But next week at AIT, it's going to be a different sheet of music."